CENTENN

D0764084

OCT - - 2009

VIDEO GAMES

Rhianna Pratchett

 Crabtree Publishing Company

www.crabtreebooks.com

Crabtree Publishing Company

www.crabtreebooks.com   1-800-387-7650

Copyright © **2009 CRABTREE PUBLISHING COMPANY**.
All rights reserved. No part of this publication may be reproduced,
stored in a retrieval system or be transmitted in any form or by
any means, electronic, mechanical, photocopying, recording, or
otherwise, without the prior written permission of Crabtree
Publishing Company.

**Published
in Canada
Crabtree Publishing**
616 Welland Ave.
St. Catharines, ON
L2M 5V6

**Published in the
United States
Crabtree Publishing**
PMB16A
350 Fifth Ave., Suite 3308
New York, NY 10118

Content development by Shakespeare Squared
www.ShakespeareSquared.com
First published in Great Britain in 2008 by ticktock Media Ltd,
2 Orchard Business Centre, North Farm Road,
Tunbridge Wells, Kent, TN2 3XF
Copyright © ticktock Entertainment Ltd 2008

Author: Rhianna Pratchett
Project editor: Ruth Owen
Project designer: Sara Greasley
Photo research: Ruth Owen
Proofreader: Crystal Sikkens
Production coordinator:
      Katherine Kantor
Prepress technician:
      Katherine Kantor

With thanks to series
editors Honor Head
and Jean Coppendale.

Thank you to Lorraine
Petersen and the
members of nasen

Picture credits:
Alamy: © Picture Contact: p. 26–27
Courtesy Ralph H. Baer: p. 6–7
© 2004-2008 Blizzard Entertainment, Inc.: cover (center left),
      13, 14–15
Courtesy Auravision, Inc.: p. 16, 17
DigiPen Institute of Technology: p. 24
© 2005-2008 Double Fine Productions: p. 2–3, 22, 23
Courtesy of EA SPORTS: cover (center right)
Getty Images: AFP: p. 4–5
Heavenly Sword™ © 2007 Sony Computer Entertainment
      Europe. Heavenly Sword is a trademark of Sony Computer
      Entertainment Europe. All rights reserved: p. 19 (bottom)
id Software: cover (top left), p. 11 (bottom)
Introversion Software: p. 28–29
Microsoft: cover (center and bottom), p. 8, 9 (top), 9 (bottom)
Rex Features: p. 19 (top); ©Paramount/Everett: p. 18
Shutterstock: cover (top center), p. 1, 8–9 (center), 21, 31 (top)
Splash Damage: p. 10, 11 (top)
Ticktock Media Archive: p. 4
© Valve Corporation. Used with Permission: p. 25

Every effort has been made to trace copyright holders, and we apologize in
advance for any omissions. We would be pleased to insert the appropriate
acknowledgments in any subsequent edition of this publication.

Library and Archives Canada Cataloguing in Publication

Pratchett, Rhianna
      Video games / Rhianna Pratchett.

(Crabtree contact)
Includes index.
ISBN 978-0-7787-3817-6 (bound).--ISBN 978-0-7787-3839-8 (pbk.)

1. Video games--Juvenile literature. I. Title. II. Series.

GV1469.3.P73 2008   j794.8   C2008-906083-0

Library of Congress Cataloging-in-Publication Data

Pratchett, Rhianna.
      Video games / Rhianna Pratchett.
            p. cm. -- (Crabtree contact)
Includes index.
ISBN-13: 978-0-7787-3839-8 (pbk. : alk. paper)
ISBN-10: 0-7787-3839-6 (pbk. : alk. paper)
ISBN-13: 978-0-7787-3817-6 (reinforced library binding : alk. paper)
ISBN-10: 0-7787-3817-5 (reinforced library binding : alk. paper)
1. Video games--Juvenile literature. I. Title. II. Series.

GV1469.3.P73 2009
794.8--dc22
                                                                2008040138

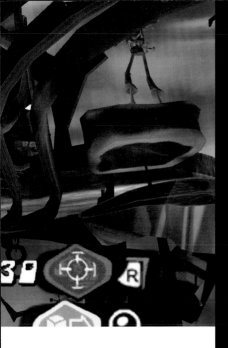

Contents

CHAPTER 1

THE BIRTH OF VIDEO GAMES

Video games have a long history that includes many kinds of games, **consoles**, and gaming styles. Did you know that the first video game, *Spacewar!* was created in 1962?

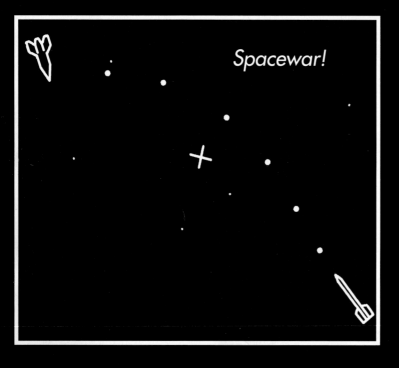

Spacewar!

Spacewar! was a basic two-player game. The **objective** was to shoot down your **opponent's** spaceship without crashing your spaceship into a big star.

People played Spacewar! on one of the first computers called a PDP1 (Programmed Data Processor 1).

Fast-forward to 2008 and the release of Nintendo's *Wii Fit*. *Wii Fit* launched a worldwide, chart-topping fitness craze.

Wii Fit requires players to move their bodies and perform exercises in order to move the characters on the screen. *Wii Fit* allows players to play games and workout at the same time.

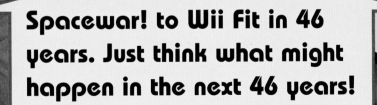

Spacewar! to Wii Fit in 46 years. Just think what might happen in the next 46 years!

CHAPTER 2

CONSOLE GAMING

In 1972, the world got its first console, the Magnavox Odyssey. A console is an electronic unit on which to play games.

The Magnavox Odyssey was designed by Ralph H. Baer. He is known as "the Grandfather of Video Games."

"Brown Box"

The "Brown Box" was the **prototype** for the Magnavox Odyssey. It may have sounded like one of the Transformers, but it finally brought video games into people's homes.

Without the Magnavox Odyssey, we may not have had an Xbox 360, a PLAYSTATION 3 (PS3), or a Nintendo Wii.

A 1972 ad for the Magnavox Odyssey

Console

Hand controller

Plug-in game programming carts

Shooting Gallery screenshots

Baer also created the first **peripheral**. It was a light gun for a Magnavox Odyssey game called *Shooting Gallery*.

CHAPTER 3

ONLINE GAMING

SEGA's Dreamcast was the first console with a built-in **modem**. This meant it could properly support online gaming.

Dreamcast made **multiplayer** games, such as *Phantasy Star Online*, extremely popular.

When Sony released a **network adapter** for the PS2, it allowed players all over the world to voice chat through a headset.

Headset

But it was not until the release of Xbox Live for Xbox and the Xbox 360, that online console gaming really took off.

Xbox Live now has over 8 million players worldwide.

Online gaming has always had a big following.

It began with games such as *Quake 3* and *Unreal Tournament*.

A Quake clan gets together to play.

These games have large groups of fans.
The fans create **forums** and **clans**.

Fans often use online tools and **editors**
to create their own "mods" (modifications),
maps, and missions for the games they love.

**Making a map or level is a great way to
learn how games are created.**

Splash Damage at work

Splash Damage is a company that develops games.

The company started out as mod-makers and fans of *Quake 3*.

In Splash Damage's latest game *Enemy Territory: Quake Wars*, players can play as a human or as an alien Strogg.

Many online gamers take part in **MMORPG**s. This stands for Massively Multiplayer Online Role-Playing Games.

MMORPG means games in which many players play together in a non-stop world.

These worlds often have fantasy themes.

Players can "level up" their characters' skills and collect new weapons and armor.

One of the most famous MMORPGs is *World of Warcraft*. It has over 10 million players.

This online game came from a famous strategy game called *Warcraft: Orcs and Humans*.

An Orc from
World of Warcraft.

In the online game of *World of Warcraft*, players create characters on either the side of the Alliance or the Horde.

Players then choose their race, such as human, undead, Draenei, or Blood elves. They also choose their class, such as a shape-changing **druid** or an axe-wielding warrior.

After that, there is the huge world of Azeroth to explore and quest through.

The Draenei are an alien race who have been at war with the race of Orcs for many years.

Online gaming is much more than just a hobby—it is an actual competitive sport known as **eSports.**

There are eSports **tournaments** all over the world. Players can win money and other prizes.

Wendel in action

One of the most famous eSportsmen is American Johnathan Wendel.

Wendel has won more major gaming tournaments than any other gamer on the planet.

Playing games is his job, so Wendel spends up to 10 hours each day playing and practicing. He also watches videos of himself in action to help him improve.

Wendel plays against students taking part in a video gaming course.

Wendel is a **spokesperson** for eSports. He also created his own range of gaming equipment.

CHAPTER 5

GAMES AND THE MOVIES

Many games have been made into movies, such as *Tomb Raider* and *Hitman*.

Not many have been very successful. However, movie-makers still want to link up with video games because games are such big business.

The most popular entertainment product ever is the video game *Grand Theft Auto IV*. This game is for mature players who are over 17. It earned over 300 million dollars in just 24 hours.

That is more than the movie *Spider-Man 3* and the book *Harry Potter and the Deathly Hallows*, earned in their first 24 hours, put together!

Angelina Jolie as a video game character Lara Croft in the movie *Tomb Raider.*

Movie-makers are also using their skills to make video games.

The actor Andy Serkis was the **dramatic director** for the PS3 exclusive *Heavenly Sword.*

He also voiced the main villain, King Bohan.

Andy Serkis played Gollum in *Lord of the Rings.*

King Bohan

CHAPTER 6

VIOLENCE IN GAMES

Violence in games is a hot topic that many people have opinions about.

In 2008, *Grand Theft Auto IV* was released in North America with a 17+ **age-rating**. The rating means the game is not appropriate for children younger than 17 years old. Games with violence, bad language, and other inappropriate content are given high age-ratings.

Many video game stores in North America and other parts of the world ask customers for identification to prove they are old enough to purchase mature games.

Violence in games—have your say...

- Is it OK to include violence in games as long as they have an age-rating?

- When people look at an age-rating, do you think they know what they might see or play in a game?

Age-ratings help us buy appropriate games.

The age-ratings are decided based on the game's content. For example, does the game show violence? Do characters use bad language?

CHAPTER 7 : MAKING GAMES

Years ago, games used to be made by just a couple of people. Now a team might include designers, artists, **programmers**, writers, and **sound engineers**.

Most games take between two and three years to develop.

One of the most important parts of designing a game is coming up with USPs (Unique Selling Points).

USPs are all the unique and exciting features that make the game stand out from other games.

These are screenshots from *Psychonauts*. One of the game's USPs is its imaginative designs for the different levels of the game.

Psychonauts is an action-adventure game. It is about a young boy named Raz and his adventures at a summer camp for kids with **psychic** powers.

Most game developers show their game's design to publishers during a "**pitch**."

If a publisher likes the idea, they will pay the developers to produce the game.

However, amazing games can come from unusual places.

Princess No Knees in *Narbacular Drop*

Narbacular Drop was a free game. It was created by students at Digipen, a college known for its game design program. The game won many awards.

Narbacular Drop features a Princess called "No Knees" because she could not jump.

When a gaming company called Valve saw the game, they liked it a lot!

The company liked it so much, they offered the students their ultimate dream gaming job— a place on Valve's team!

A screenshot from *Portal*

Valve remade the game as Portal—one of the best action-puzzle games ever!

During a game's development, the design team continues to design the gameplay.

They design things such as missions, boss fights, and even combat.

Artists create the game's visuals. They create everything from characters to textures, such as bricks.

Programmers create the game's "engine." This makes all the parts of a game run together.

Sound engineers and composers create the sound effects and music.

Writers write the game's story and the characters' speech.

Testers play-test the game. They make sure the game is working properly.

When the game is finished, developers say it has "gone gold."

An artist at work

It is getting easier for small development teams to release games.

Xbox LIVE Market Place and Valve's Steam mean games can be released without having a big team and spending a lot of money.

Valve's Steam allows people to buy and download games onto their computers.

Working on *Uplink*

Packing games

The gaming company Introversion Software was started by three university friends. They created a game called *Uplink*. They did all the work—even packing up the games to mail to customers!

Their second game, *Darwinia*, was bought by Steam. Steam helped Introversion get money to create new games.

Introversion is now a team of 11 people. They say Steam helped to make their company a success.

Darwinia's look and level design recreates the look of old arcade games such as *Space Invaders*.

NEED-TO-KNOW WORDS

age-rating A rating and symbol given to a video game to tell buyers for which age level the game is suitable

clan A team of players who game together

console An electronic unit on which to play games

dramatic director A person in charge of directing the voice actors in a game

druid A mystical person from an ancient Celtic religion

editor A piece of software which allows you to design a game or parts of a game

eSports Video games played as a professional sport

forum The place on a gaming website where players can chat with each other

MMORPG (Massively Multiplayer Online Role-Playing Game) A role-playing game played online with many players

modem A device for sending electronic data

multiplayer The part of a game that can be played by many players at once

network adapter A device to connect a computer to other computers in a network for high speed communication

objective A goal

opponent Someone who you play a game against

peripheral A device, such as a steering wheel, that can be plugged into a console and used to control a game

pitch To suggest an idea or solution

programmer A person who writes computer programs

prototype The first model or design of something

psychic A person with special powers, such as the ability to read minds or see into the future

sound engineer A person who controls and monitors the sound for a video game

spokesperson A person who speaks on behalf of someone else

tournament A big competition

GET INTO MAKING GAMES

If you are interested in making games, the International Game Developers Association website has some helpful advice: *http://www.igda.org/breakingin/* There are many roles in game development, each with their own skills. But you do not have to be a big team to create great games. Get involved with online gaming communities and take part in modifications and map-making. Who knows? You might create the next *Narbacular Drop*.

Good luck!

Before visiting an online gaming community, you must first get permission from a parent or caregiver. Never give personal information such as your address, telephone number, or the name of your school, to anyone online.

VIDEO GAMES ONLINE

www.howstuffworks.com/video-game.htm
Learn how video game systems are made

www.pbs.org/kcts/videogamerevolution/
Explore the history of video games

www.esrb.org/ratings/ratings_guide.jsp
Find information on the Entertainment Software Rating Board (ESRB)

INDEX